Southwood Elementary School Library

W9-CCF-859

50

Pumpernickel Tickle and Mean Green Cheese

PUMPERNICKEL TICKLE AND MEAN GREEN CHEESE

by Nancy Patz

Franklin Watts
New York|London|1978

Library of Congress Cataloging in Publication Data

Patz, Nancy.
  Pumpernickel tickle and mean green cheese.

  SUMMARY: Benjamin and Elephant are sent to
the store to buy some groceries but Elephant makes
so many rhymes and puns on the list that they forget
what they are supposed to buy.
  [1. Humorous stories] I. Title.
PZ7.P27833Pu   [E]   78-2915
ISBN 0-531-02221-8 (lib. bdg.)
      0-531-02492-X

Copyright © 1978 by Nancy Patz Blaustein • All rights reserved • Printed in the United States of America
5   4   3   2

To Fanny, Harry, Biddy, and Hilda

One morning Benjamin and Elephant were busy as usual.

Benjamin's mother came in and said, "Benjamin,
please go and buy a loaf of dark brown pumpernickel bread,
and a half-pound piece of yellow cheese,
and a great big, very green, nice dill pickle.

"Now try to remember, Benjamin. You always seem to
forget something."

"I promise I won't forget a thing," said Benjamin.
"Come with me, El?"

"Okay, Benj," said Elephant.

They walked and talked together.

Benjamin said, "A loaf of dark brown pumpernickel bread,
and a half-pound piece of yellow cheese,
and a great big, very green, nice dill pickle."

"Yellow cheese and belly-squeeze," said Elephant.
"Pumpernickel-bumperstickle. Half-pound, half-round
pumpernickel-tickle."

And Benjamin laughed.

But he was afraid he might forget
what he was supposed to remember.
So he said, "Stop it, El."
"Okay, Benj," said Elephant.
And on they went together.

Benjamin said, "Dark brown pumpernickel, half-pound
yellow cheese, great big, very green, nice dill pickle."
"Pick-a-pack-of-pickle-nickels," said Elephant.
And he walked a little faster and said a little louder,
"Pick-a-pack-of-chickadees. Pack-a-peck-of-bumblebees.
Big-brown, up-down, lick-a-nickel-tickle."
And Benjamin laughed.

But he was afraid he might forget
what he was supposed to remember.
So he said, "Stop it, El! Be sensible."
"Okay, Benj," said Elephant.
And on they went together.

Benjamin walked faster and said a little louder,
"Dark brown pumpernickel. Half-pound yellow peas.
Great big, very green, nice dill tickle.

"Oh, no!" said Benjamin. "What am I saying?"
And Elephant laughed.

Elephant said, "Pickle-tickle."
Benjamin said, "Tickle-nickel."
"Half-pound."
"Half-round."
"Mean green cheese."
They laughed all the way to the grocery.

Southwood Elementary School Library

But when they got there,
they couldn't remember a thing!

They stared and stared at the grocery man.

"I told you to be sensible. Now you made us forget!" hissed Benjamin.

"Don't worry, Benj, I'll remember. I'm always good at remembering," Elephant bragged.

He took a big deep breath.

And he said in a big loud voice,

"Mr. Grocery Man, Sir, we would like a . . .

dark brown belly-tickle.

And a half-pound bumperstickle.

And a very nice, *very* nice, great big
mean green SNEEZE, please!"

And they laughed and laughed
until their stomachs hurt.
Benjamin bumped into Elephant
who stumbled and tumbled and
almost got stuck in the pickle barrel!

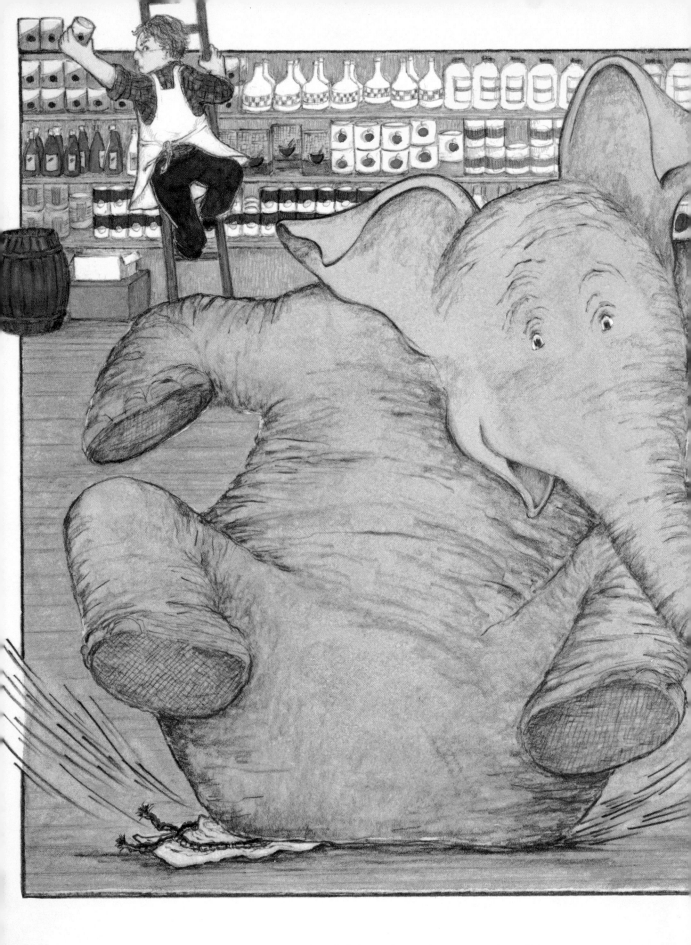

Then he crashed like thunder on the floor.

"What was that?" the grocery man grumbled as the whole place shook.

Benjamin helped Elephant up. "You did too forget," he said.

"Elephants never forget. I just got mixed up, that's all," Elephant huffed.

"We've got to try to remember, El," said Benjamin.

"Okay, Benj," said Elephant.

So they looked at all the food on the shelves and tried to remember.

"Hey, Benj," asked Elephant, "did we come to buy some peanuts?
Or hot dogs with mustard? Or barbecued custard?
A hot chicken noodle? A fat pickled poodle?"
"I'm telling you, Elephant, cut it out!" yelled Benjamin.

"Cut-cut-cut and tut-tut-tut," Elephant called
as he danced around.

"You're not funny," yelled Benjamin.

"I'm a funny-honey-bunny," Elephant teased.

"You're not!"
yelled Benjamin.
"You're a hunk-a-bunk-
with-a-big-fat-trunk."
That made Elephant angry.
"Well, you're a
hunk-a-punkle-pickle,"
yelled Elephant.

"Hunk-a-punkle."
"Pickle-punkle."

"Pickle-jelly."
"Tickle-belly."

"Tickle-punkle."
"Pickle-punkle."
"Mean-green-fleas!"

And they sounded so silly they burst out laughing.

"El, you're no help at all," said Benjamin. "Did we come to buy some soup?"

"No, I really don't think so," said Elephant.

"Milk or meat or butter or bread?" asked Benjamin.

And then he stopped.

"Bread!" he yelled at Elephant. "Pumpernickel bread!"

"DARK BROWN PUMPERNICKEL. HALF-POUND YELLOW CHEESE. GREAT BIG, VERY GREEN, NICE DILL PICKLE."

They shouted it proudly together and marched to tell the grocery man.

The two friends hurried so they would be home
by lunchtime.

"Pumpernickel-tickle-pickle," said Benjamin.

Elephant said, "Pick-a-pack-of-pickle-peas."

"Pick-a-pack-of-pumpernickels," said Benjamin.
Elephant said, "Pickle-tickle, bumperstickle.
Pumpernickel-picklecheese."

And that's the way they talked...

all the way home.

"Good for you, Benjamin," said Benjamin's mother.
"You remembered everything I wanted."

Elephant smiled at Benjamin, and Benjamin smiled back.

Guess what they had for lunch!

3